Dinosaurs

What Were Dinosaurs?

Rebecca Rissman

 Raintree

www.raintreepublishers.co.uk
Visit our website to find out more information about Raintree books.

To order:
☎ Phone 0845 6044371
▤ Fax +44 (0) 1865 312263
▤ Email myorders@raintreepublishers.co.uk

Customers from outside the UK please telephone +44 1865 312262

Raintree is an imprint of Capstone Global Library Limited, a company incorporated in England and Wales having its registered office at 7 Pilgrim Street, London, EC4V 6LB – Registered company number: 6695582

Edited by Rebecca Rissman, Siân Smith, Charlotte Guillain, and Vaarunika Dharmapala
Designed by Kimberly Miracle
Original illustrations © Capstone Global Library Ltd 2010
Illustrated by Maureen and Gordon Gray, James Field, and Darren Lingard
Picture research by Tracy Cummins and Kim Tidwell
Originated by Steve Walker, Capstone Global Library Ltd
Printed and bound in China by Leo Paper Products Ltd

ISBN 978 0 431194 37 0 (hardback)
14 13 12 11 10
10 9 8 7 6 5 4 3 2

British Library Cataloguing in Publication Data
Rissman, Rebecca.
   What were dinosaurs?. -- (Acorn plus)
   1. Dinosaurs--Juvenile literature.
   I. Title II. Series
   567.9-dc22

Acknowledgements
We would like to thank the following for permission to reproduce photographs: Corbis **pp. 8, 9 right, 20, 21** (© all Science Faction/Louie Psihoyos); Getty Images **pp. 4** (DEA Picture Library), **6** (Visuals Unlimited/Ken Lucas), **7 left** (Discovery Channel Images/Jeff Foott); Photolibrary **p. 7 right** (Index Stock Photography/Melba Photo Agency); Shutterstock **p.5** (© Chee-Onn Leong), **7 center** (© Paul Maguire); Superstock **pp. 9 left** (© George Ostertag), **11 right** and **12**.

Cover photograph of a *Tyrannosaurus rex* reproduced with permission of Shutterstock/© fotoadamczyk.

We would like to thank Nancy Harris and Adriana Scalise for their invaluable help in the preparation of this book.

Every effort has been made to contact copyright holders of material reproduced in this book. Any omissions will be rectified in subsequent printings if notice is given to the publishers.

Contents

Some words are shown in bold, **like this**. They are explained in "Words to Know" on page 23.

What were dinosaurs?

Dinosaurs were animals that lived long ago. Dinosaurs were **reptiles**. Dinosaurs lived all over Earth.

The plants and animals on Earth change over time. The dinosaurs that were around long ago are now **extinct**. Animals and plants that are extinct are not living any more.

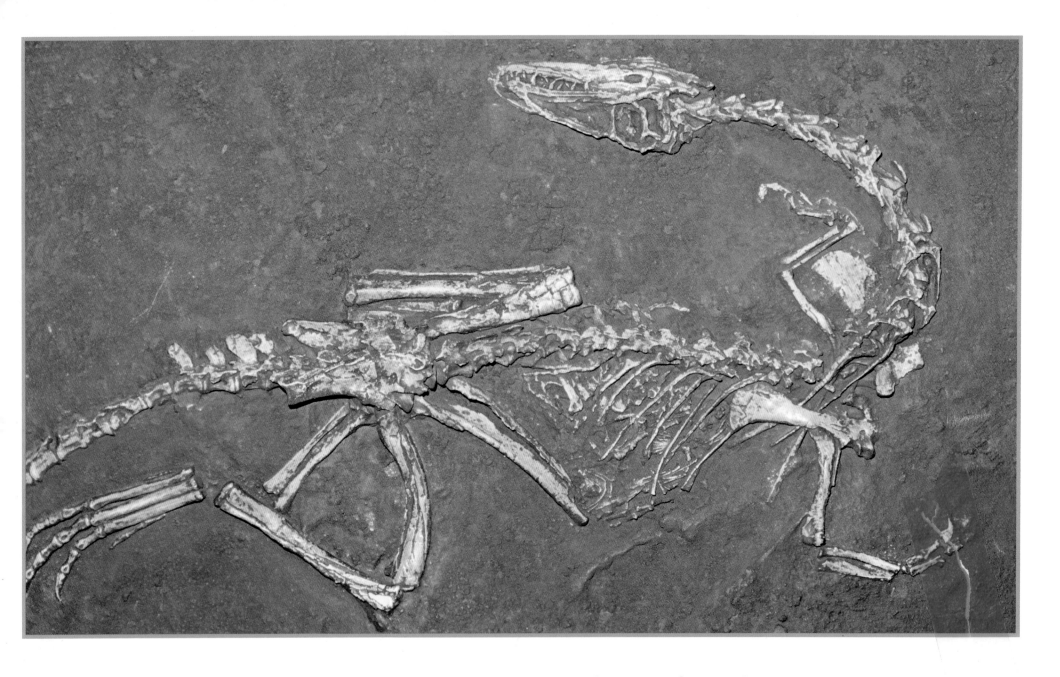

We can learn about **dinosaurs** from **fossils**. Fossils are parts of plants or animals that lived long ago. Fossils are found in rocks.

plant	animal	insect

Fossils can be plants. Fossils can be animals.
Fossils can be insects. We can learn about the past
from fossils.

Fossils can show us what life was like on Earth long ago. Fossils can tell us how life has changed over time.

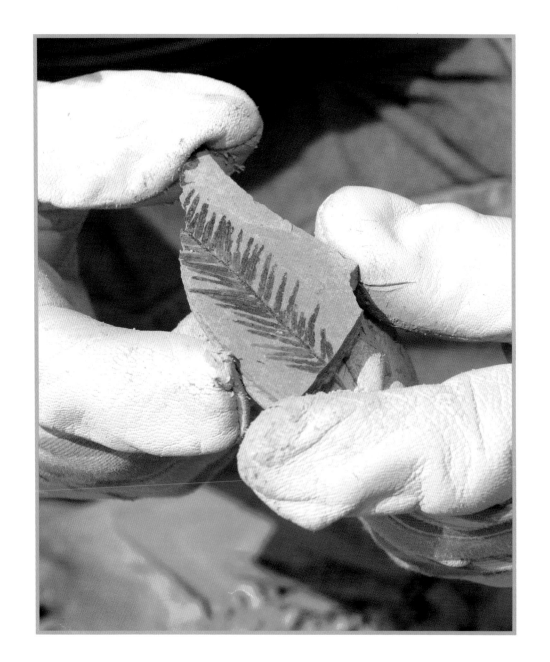

Some fossils are small and **delicate**. Other fossils are very large.

Different dinosaurs

Dinosaurs lived on Earth for a very long time. There were many different types of dinosaurs.

Some dinosaurs lived on land. Some dinosaurs spent time in water.

Dinosaurs could look very different. Some **dinosaurs** had very long necks. *Brontosaurus* used its neck to reach tall leaves.

plates

Dinosaurs had different **body coverings**. Some dinosaurs were covered with **scales**. Some dinosaurs had large **plates** on their bodies. Other dinosaurs were covered with feathers, like birds!

Dinosaur diets

Triceratops

Some **dinosaurs** ate plants. *Triceratops* was a dinosaur that ate plants. It had three long spikes on its head for **protection**.

Brachiosaurus

Brachiosaurus was a dinosaur that ate plants. But *Brachiosaurus* also ate rocks! These rocks helped it to **digest** or break down its food.

Some **dinosaurs** ate other animals. *Velociraptor* was a dinosaur that ate other animals. *Velociraptor* was a good **hunter**.

The pterodactyl was a flying **reptile** that ate insects. The pterodactyl could fly high in the air.

Live alone or together?

Some **dinosaurs** lived in groups. They ate or hunted together. *Diplodocus* lived in groups for **protection**.

Some dinosaurs lived alone. *Tyrannosaurus rex* may have lived alone.

Learning about dinosaurs

Scientists study **dinosaur fossils**. They search for fossils around the world.

Fossils can show what dinosaurs ate. Fossils can show how dinosaurs lived. Fossils can even show how some dinosaurs became **extinct**.

Body coverings

Dinosaurs had different **body coverings**. Do you remember what these body coverings are called?

1

2

3

Answers on page 24.

Words to know

body covering	material the body is covered in. For example, an animal's body might be covered with skin or fur.
delicate	breaks easily. We have to handle delicate things carefully to keep them from breaking.
digest	break down food into small pieces so that the body can use it
dinosaur	a reptile that lived millions of years ago
extinct	no longer exists because every animal of that kind has died
fossil	parts of a dead plant or animal that has become hard like rock
hunter	an animal that catches other animals for food
plate	a thin, flat, hard material
protection	keeping safe
reptile	a cold-blooded animal. Snakes, lizards, turtles, and alligators are reptiles.
scale	small, hard plate that covers an animal's body

Index

Note to parents and teachers

Before reading:

Begin building background knowledge by asking children the following questions: What does a dinosaur look like? Are there different types of dinosaurs? What did dinosaurs eat? Does anyone know what "extinct" means? Ask children to share what they know about dinosaurs with a partner. Explain to children that they will learn about fossils and how they give scientists a lot of information about dinosaurs' existence and extinction.

After reading:

• Help children to write a poem about dinosaurs either independently or as a whole class exercise. This could be a four-line poem that follows the following pattern: line 1 is a describing word, line 2 is the name of the dinosaur, line 3 describes an action, and line 4 describes a feeling or how it looks. Alternatively you could create a poem where the letters at the start of each line of the poem together spell the word *dinosaur* (acrostic poetry).

• Ask children to find out about their favourite dinosaur. Create a sheet with a list of questions that children can fill out at home or during a library visit, or decide what the important questions are together. Children can report back on their findings.

Answers to questions on page 22

Picture 1 shows scales. Picture 2 shows plates. Picture 3 shows feathers.